Gina & Jo

Welcome to London!

Lila & I will probably be having about town when you arrive, but we have reservations for 7°° p.m. for dinner, if you're rested. Tomorrow (Thurs) Hugh Donald will also be in town. Please leave a message for Rm. 505

x xx Mike

thelwell's.
Compleat Tangler

thelwell's
Compleat
Tangler

Being a Pictorial Discourse of

ANGLERS and ANGLING

METHUEN & C? LTD

First published in 1967
Reprinted in 1968 *and* 1971
by Methuen & Co Ltd
Copyright © 1967 by Norman Thelwell
Printed in Great Britain by
John Dickens & Co Ltd Northampton
SBN 416 46380 0
1·4

Contents

Angler's Glory

THERE ARE MANY REASONS WHY MEN GO FISHING

FOR SOME IT MEANS ESCAPE FROM THE NOISE AND TURMOIL OF EVERYDAY LIFE

FOR OTHERS, IT IS A CHANGE FROM THE MONOTONY
OF SITTING ON AN OFFICE STOOL ALL DAY

SOME REGARD ANGLING AS AN EXACT SCIENCE

OTHERS ARE DRAWN BY
ITS EXCITING UNCERTAINTIES

BUT FOR MOST MEN IT IS THE LOVE OF A FRESH WIND ON THE FACE

AND THE ENCHANTING SOUND OF RUNNING WATER

IT IS THE PRIMITIVE JOY OF HUNTING WILD CREATURES

OF PITTING HIS OWN WITS AGAINST THEIR NATURAL CUNNING

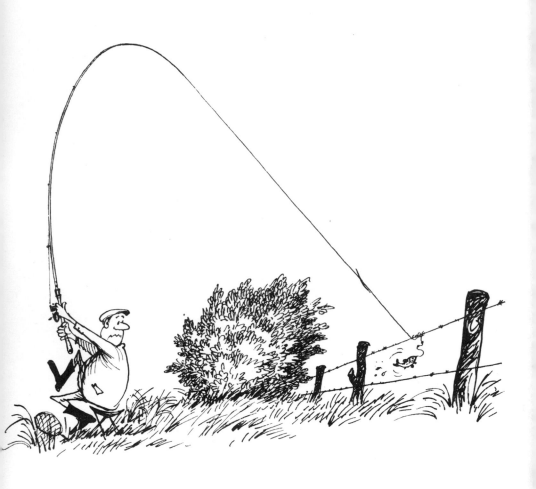

AND OVERCOMING THEIR RESISTANCE BY SHEER SKILL

WHEN FISH ARE ON THE FEED —

THERE IS NOTHING QUITE LIKE THE SUPPRESSED EXCITEMENT

OF TACKLING UP —

— OF SELECTING EXACTLY THE RIGHT BAIT —

— OF FEELING THE BALANCE AND WHIP OF A FAVOURITE ROD

AND MAKING THE FIRST CAST

THE EXPERIENCED ANGLER IS PREPARED FOR LITTLE SNAGS OF COURSE
AND KNOWS THE MOST SCIENTIFIC WAY TO DEAL WITH THEM

HALF HIS PLEASURE LIES IN MANIPULATING HIS BELOVED TACKLE

... AND SOLVING TECHNICAL PROBLEMS

BUT ONCE HIS TACKLE IS AMONG THE FISH —

HE IS THE HAPPIEST OF MEN

HE CAN SAVOUR THE STRANGE THRILL OF BEING UTTERLY ALONE ...

... TINGLE TO THE SHARP EXCITEMENT OF THE DAY'S FIRST BITE ...

... AND KNOW THE SATISFACTION OF MAKING A SUCCESSFUL STRIKE

HE CAN LEAN BACK IN CONTENTMENT ON COWSLIP BANKS

AND LET EVERYTHING WASH OVER HIM

*   *   *

FOR NATURE IS EVERYWHERE ABOUT HIM

FOR COMPANY –
HE HAS THE FRIENDLY, SHORTSIGHTED LITTLE WATER VOLE

AND NATURE'S OWN ANGLERS TO ADMIRE

WHO BUT HE KNOWS THE HAUNTING BOOM OF THE BITTERN —

AND THE MUSIC OF THE MUTE SWAN'S WING ?

HIS DAYS ARE SPENT AMONG THE PURPLE LOOSESTRIFE AND WILD IRIS ....

HE IS FAMILIAR WITH THE SILENT SWOOP OF THE EVENING BAT

AND THE MATING DANCE OF THE BLUE WINGED OLIVES IN THE GLOAMING

HE KNOWS THE RIPPLING SHALLOWS ...

... AND DEEP POOLS

UNSELFISH BY NATURE —
HE DELIGHTS TO SHOW THE NOVICE WHERE THE BIG CHUB CRUISE ...

.... AND WHERE THE BEST PIKE LIE

AND, WHEN HE LANDS A FISH, HE WILL RARELY KILL IT —
BUT WILL WATCH IT RETURN TO THE WATER ...

HAPPY TO SEE IT FREE ONCE MORE

TO GIVE SPORT TO SOME BROTHER ANGLER

Brothers of the Angle

FISHERMEN THINK OF THEMSELVES AS ONE BIG FAMILY —

AND TREAT EACH OTHER ACCORDINGLY

THEY HAVE EVOLVED OVER THE YEARS INTO THREE
DISTINCT SPECIES

THE LARGEST OF THESE IS THE COARSE FISHERMAN

HE IS HAPPY TO TAKE ALMOST ANY KIND OF FISH....

FROM ANY KIND OF WATER

HE COLLECTS A WIDE RANGE OF TACKLE

AND KNOWS PRECISELY HOW TO USE IT

HE IS A GREAT BELIEVER IN SPECIALLY PREPARED BAITS

HIS RANKS HAVE DIVIDED INTO THREE SUB-SPECIES :-

(1)   THE SERIOUS MATCH ANGLER ———

INTERESTED IN NOTHING BUT CATCHING FISH

(2) THE SOLITARY "PLEASURE" FISHERMAN

WHOSE ONE DESIRE —

IS TO GET AWAY FROM IT ALL

AND (3) THE SPECIMEN HUNTER

CONTENT TO WAIT WEEKS FOR HIS QUARRY . . .

. . . AND CONTEMPTUOUS OF ANYTHING . . . .

... WHICH DOES NOT BREAK A RECORD

The Game Men

THE MOST EXCLUSIVE OF ALL ANGLERS IS THE DRY FLY MAN

HE LIKES TO STUDY THE RIVER FROM A BENTLEY

AND IS INTERESTED ONLY IN WATER AS CLEAR AS GIN

— AND TWICE AS EXPENSIVE

HE PUTS A LORRY LOAD OF TROUT INTO HIS WATER EVERY SPRING

AND EMPLOYS EXPERTS TO ENSURE THAT THEY NEVER GET OUT

HE SPENDS MANY HOURS STUDYING
MINUTE AQUATIC FLIES ....

... WHICH HIS TROUT VERY RARELY EAT

AND TYING IMITATIONS — WHICH LOOK NOTHING LIKE THE REAL ONES

HE CAN IDENTIFY A FLY TAKEN BY A TROUT —
AT FIFTY YARDS RANGE

AND WEARS SPECIAL DARK GLASSES TO DO IT ——

BUT HE CANNOT SEE AN IMITATION TWELVE INCHES AWAY

FISHING IS HIS SOLE FORM OF EXERCISE — BUT HE
CONSIDERS IT BAD FORM TO MOVE MORE THAN HIS
WRIST WHEN CASTING

HE HOOKS HIS FAVOURITE FLIES CONVENIENTLY INTO HIS TWEED CLOTHING –

– WHERE NOTHING CAN REMOVE THEM WHEN NEEDED ——

... EXCEPT THE WIND

THE WET FLY MAN IS A MORE ACTIVE CREATURE

AND SPENDS A GOOD DEAL OF TIME IN THE WATER

HE IS LESS VAIN ABOUT HIS APPEARANCE

HE RARELY SEES HIS FISH UNTIL HE HAS HOOKED IT

UNLIKE **THE SALMON MAN**

SALMON DO NOT FEED IN FRESH WATER.
SO THE ANGLER'S ONLY HOPE IS TO AGGRAVATE THEM

NEVER THE LESS - THE SALMON EXERTS A PARTICULARLY STRONG HOLD —

— ON ITS ADHERENTS . . . . .

AND IT IS FREQUENTLY TAKEN ON BOTH FLY AND SPINNER

The Sea Anglers

THESE HARDY FISHERMEN ENJOY ONE OF THE MOST EXCITING
AND INVIGORATING SPORTS IN THE WORLD

THERE IS A WARM FEELING OF BROTHERHOOD AMONG ALL
THOSE WHO LOVE MESSING ABOUT IN BOATS ———

BUT ONE MAY SPEND MANY HOURS AFLOAT WITHOUT SEEING ANOTHER HUMAN BEING

THE SEA ANGLER LIKES TO DIG HIS OWN BAIT WHENEVER POSSIBLE

AND TO LEARN AT FIRST HAND THE
INTRICACIES OF TIDES AND CURRENTS

HE HAS HIS OWN PECULIAR PROBLEMS

WHETHER CASTING FROM THE BEACH —

OR FROM A BOAT

FOR SUCCESSFUL SEA FISHING THE TYPE OF TACKLE MUST BE
APPROPRIATE TO THE KIND OF FISH ONE WISHES TO CATCH

...ND WARM SENSIBLE CLOTHING IS VITAL FOR FULL ENJOYMENT OF THE SPORT

A KNOWLEDGE OF WHERE THE FISH ARE LIKELY TO BE LOCATED
CAN SAVE HOURS OF FRUSTRATION

AND THE ABILITY TO HANDLE THE CATCH IS ESSENTIAL

THE BEST PLACES TO FISH MAY BE LEARNED BY WATCHING THE EXPERTS...

—THEY HAVE AN UNCANNY ABILITY TO LOCATE FISH

FULL USE SHOULD BE MADE OF SEA OBJECTS PUT THERE FOR YOUR CONVENIENCE

AND IT IS ADVISABLE TO UNDERSTAND THE LANGUAGE OF THE SEA

WHEN AFTER REALLY BIG FISH, THE LINE MUST BE STRONG ENOUGH TO AVOID BREAKAGES

AND ABOVE ALL —

WATCH OUT FOR SIGNS OF BAD WEATHER

GETTING A BOAT HOME IN ADVERSE CONDITIONS —

CAN PROVE VERY TRICKY

Some Technical Terms Explained

A SLIPPING CLUTCH

HOOK TO GUT

A BLOODY BUTCHER

RIVER REPORT

BLEAK

TROTTING

THE WATER

SWAN SHOT

A SALMON LIE

Nº 2 HOOK

FISH'S WINDOW

LOB WORM

BLUE UPRIGHT

PALE WATERY

A DISGORGER

MILLER'S THUMB

SURF CASTING

HAIRY MARY

TERMINAL TACKLE

Angler's Etiquette

NEVER BEGRUDGE SPECTATORS THEIR INTEREST IN YOUR PISCATORIAL PROWESS

ON NO ACCOUNT TRAMPLE GROWING CROPS —

OR CAUSE ANNOYANCE TO FARM ANIMALS

BE PREPARED TO LISTEN TO THE OPINIONS OF OTHER ANGLERS

AND TO GIVE THEM THE BENEFIT OF YOUR OWN EXPERIENCE IN RETURN

IT IS UNFORGIVABLE TO IMPEDE A FELLOW ANGLER . . . . .

. . . . . WHO IS TRYING TO LAND A FISH . . .

... OR TO LEAVE LITTER ABOUT AFTER A DAY'S PLEASURE

AND FINALLY ———

IF YOU THINK YOU HAVE
CAUGHT A RECORD FISH....

.... MAKE SURE YOU HAVE A WITNESS ....

AND ON NO ACCOUNT DISPOSE OF IT UNTIL ALL NECESSARY FACTS HAVE BEEN VERIFIED